DON'T SAY NO FOR THE PROSPECT

How I Went from a Sales Rookie to a Retail Leasing Rockstar to a Shopping Center Owner with $79 Million in Assets

By Beth Azor

with Jill Ratzan

ISBN (978-0-578-21249-4)

Printed in USA by Instant Publisher.

Companies Beth Has Worked With
(In the Last 18 Months)

Fresh Kitchen
Select Comfort
Kirklands
Panera Bread
Burger 21
Dunkin Donuts
Walmart
Ross Dress For Less
7-11
Sherwin Williams
Wing Stop
United Healthcare
Starbucks
Mission BBQ
Blaze Pizza
Aldi
Verizon Wireless
DXL Men's Apparel
Amscot
MD Now Urgent Care

Contents

> *"It takes a village."*
> AFRICAN PROVERB

Acknowledgements

Please bear with me: this book is 14 years in the making, and I have a lot of people to thank!

As a single mom of two boys and working two jobs I have most definitely relied on my village a lot over the years. "It takes a village" certainly takes on new meaning as I stop and try to acknowledge everyone who has played a part in my success and in this book. Please forgive me if I haven't specifically named you here; may you still feel my appreciation regardless.

In chronological order (more or less)...

Mom and Dad, obviously without you I wouldn't be here. I miss you dearly. My Dad, the ever dreamer and fearless cold caller; and my Mom, her work ethic was unbelievable. Their two quotes (gifts) to me:

Dad: "God gave you two ears and one mouth. Listen twice as much as you speak."

Mom: "Don't wait for your boss to tell you what to do. Find something that needs doing, and do it!"

Both quotes have served me well.

To those who gave me the start, including:

Susie Hazzi, who in 1986, gave me this infamous advice, "You should go into Commercial Real Estate." Donna Abood, my FSU sorority sista, who hired me at Terranova Corporation in 1986. Tom Hopkins, my first ever sales guru/mentor. I used my

7

credit card to buy his sales system. It was $3,000; I was making $18,000. I wore those cassettes out—totally worth it.

Stephen H. Bittel—what this man has done for my career and for me has no bounds. He had NO glass ceiling whatsoever. Whatever I wanted to try, he supported. He even co-signed a $50,000 loan for me so that I could make my very first retail investment. Without his tutelage at Terranova for 18 years, I would not have had this career.

My executive team at Terranova, including Laurie Rozen and Adrienne Kelly, you were and continue to be the wind beneath my wings!

I'm grateful for the commitment and trust of all of my real estate partners, including Barry Belmont, my very first coaching client and now my fabulous partner in multiple real estate projects. Your unquestionable support and respect has helped me in so many ways.

Thank you to my WIRE group (the Women in Real Estate), especially Anne Fetherston (RIP) and Melody Spano who thought every idea that I had was crazy, but after some consideration, they supported me with everything that they had.

Thank you Ivy, my BFF, for being the sounding board of my life!

Thank you to my post-college roomie, Janet Pappas, who watched me go from an $11,000 salary at the American Heart Association to being my partner in real estate deals today (and all the borrowing back and forth on a handshake!).

I am grateful to my clients and students who are too many to name, except for: DLC, Daniel Taub, Chris Ressa (hired me to canvass with his team in over 8 markets), Phillips Edison, Shopping Center Group, Equity One, Ramco Gershenson, Aaron Zucker, Andrew Fisch, Natalie Battisti, Freddy Battisti, and Alex Munoz, a former student and employee who hired me for my first keynote gig. Andrea Blade who said, "You should coach people. I'd hire and pay you to coach me." Steve Maestas, NAI Albuquerque, who came up to me after one of my workshops in 2016 and said, "When's the book coming out?" And, Laura Lynch O'Connor, who said, "If you are not scared, you're not growing!".

Thanks to all of my tenants, and to all of the many authors and leaders who have inspired and motivated me, including Gary Vaynerchuk and Grant Cardone. I'm a self-proclaimed and proud self-improvement junkie. I own it! Thank you Jill R., my co-writer, without whom this would have NEVER happened. You are brilliant and amazingly in my head! I think it and my words come out of you as if I had said them. You are the most talented, creative writer ever.

And last, but not least, my inner circle. It does, indeed, take a village!

Lea Lancourt, you are the epitome of that village—the person who is always there for my boys and me, and who never "kills my dreams!"

Alex and Mario, you both are the lights of my life. Without your laughter, hugs, high fives and hi-jinx, my life would be empty! You both complete me!

And then there's one…

To Josee Crosbie, you have been with me since the beginning, 14 years ago. The first day I met you, I said, "I want to write a book." Finally. You are definitely the yin to my yang. I am the dreamer; Josee, you are the doer! Without you I could never have accomplished all of the goals that I've set.

Thank you, Josee and everyone else for helping me on this journey.

More to come!

Foreword by Jill Ratzan
On How This Book Came to Be

I met Beth about 14 years ago. I was trying to become the next great retailer, and I was failing at it... *I mean epically.*

At the time Beth had just purchased her first shopping center. I bumped into her at a new fast-casual lunch spot that she was canvassing. We had mutual friends so we began chatting in line. In that 5-minute exchange, Beth saved both my store and my sanity.

She needed to write this book then.

See, Beth is not only brilliant, she's also honest... and persistent. And she's curious (maybe pathologically so). She asks direct, but always important questions. She is also completely real... oh, and did I mention that Beth is brilliant?

People are drawn to Beth. If you meet her, you'll want to get to know her. If you're an acquaintance, you want to become her friend. If you have a business, you want Beth as your partner; and as I know first-hand, if you have a problem, you want Beth as an advisor.

She reads every sales book she finds and literally devours the information. She listens, too. Her car is a virtual self-improvement, B-School library. The woman plays and takes notes on audio books whenever en route anywhere. (Hey Beth, two hands on the wheel please... safety first, right?!)

The best news for us is she shares!

Beth is a sought after speaker, coach and sales trainer. She runs a huge and national book club which is often attended by the writer being featured.

(Side note: She gets these famous authors to show up because she asks. Beth doesn't say no for anyone anymore.)

I knew after our first lunch-line encounter that Beth had at least one great book in her, and I wasn't the only one. After seeing Beth give a talk, newly appointed Kansas City Federal Reserve Chair and Founder of Albuquerque's NAI Maestas & Ward, Steve Maestas, asked Beth to write this book... That was 3 years ago.

So, what took her so long?

Beth was understandably hesitant. What could she possibly write in this book that hasn't already been written?

At least that's the summary of her response when I first suggested that she write one. "Who'd want to read it?"

C'mon, Beth, **don't say *"NO"* for the prospect**! I would read it; so would countless others.

That's because Beth, and hence this book, is unique in two ways: the first is that she is truly in it to help others – —Beth's approach to business is very much a team (actually a league) game... She says and acts as if her own success is dependent on the success of everyone in her universe, including her competitors.

Second, Beth says and acts as if you learn as much from your mistakes as you do from your successes, and thus she is transparent about both. In the very beginning, you'll read about what happened when she totally dismissed one of the biggest business icons in Florida.

Notice I said that Beth 'says and acts'. This is a clue as to why Beth's advice is so relatable ——all of her guidance is real-life based, field-tested, and actionable. In other words, what she says will work for anyone who works it... as it did for me.

Enjoy!!

Jill Ratzan, Weston, FL 2018

Introduction + What You'll Find
Inside This Book

Dear Reader and Friend,

Did you know that the average person reads only one book per year, *but the average chief executive reads 60?*

This particular book is written for both.

It's meant to be read and then re-read at any time.

You can absorb it all in one sitting, in sequence, or call upon a particular section in real-time as needed - think 'field manual' as opposed to textbook.

This book is intentionally conversational, but still meaty (full of worksheets, checklists, and templates). I hope that you'll feel like you're sitting in one of my Rockstar workshops, except that you can experience it from your home and in your PJs.

And after you're through with it, I want this copy to be dog-eared, highlighted, and underlined!

The book is divided into three sections, each filled with personal stories and pragmatic advice that will resonate equally, whether you're fresh out of school, a real estate rookie, a mid-career rockstar, or a grizzled real estate vet (like me).

In the first three chapters, I introduce you to the inner workings of the ***Don't Say NO For The Prospect*** (as in, "*on behalf of*") philosophy and explain how it came to be (in painful personal detail).

You'll love reading in Chapter 2 about how I totally screwed up one phone call, and how it forever changed the way I think about my prospects (for the better).

You might be surprised when you read this part to learn all the ways we give in to fear and say no for someone else.

Chapters 4–7 are where I showcase and then demonstrate the types of things that I have done and continue to do to avoid inadvertently saying *"NO"* for my prospects.

For example, in Chapter 4, I talk about the one question that you should NEVER ask when you canvass. It's a question that 99% of leasing agents always ask.

Chapter 5 is absolute required reading for anyone who hates to cold call, and for the 98% of you who DON'T CANVASS. In it, you'll find a perfect blend of actionable information and tough love (yeah, you get a gentle kick in the a$$) to get you out of your office and onto the street this week!

Actually, throughout the entire book, you get ALL of the practical things that I do when prospecting. Well, at least the ones that have consistently returned great results for my students and me.

Some examples:

• You'll get the 17 things that National Retailers told me will make them BEG YOU for a meeting. Yes, I asked them. *Here's a hint: If you want to land a meeting at ICSC, DO*

THIS—send a LinkedIn message. NOT THIS—send out an email blast.

• You get the same canvassing plan and tips that have helped hundreds of the agents that I've trained boost their response rates by as much as 30%.

• You'll also learn MY definition of a "qualified" prospect and the exact questions I ask (on the first call) to determine which businesses are the real deal and which are just fake news.

Throughout this section, you'll find dozens of call out boxes with my favorite resources and valuable lessons from my personal experience. These are key nuggets that you can use right away.

Chapter 8 is a HUGE reality check and covers what to do when things aren't going as planned. Trust me, I've been there! In this chapter, you get my advice to the most common questions I hear. I call this the "Hey Beth" section, as in, "Hey Beth, help! I can't get retailers to respond to me!" Or, "Hey Beth, help! I can't get my boss to be realistic about rates!" In this chapter, I give you insightful and detailed answers to help you navigate the obstacles that can befuddle and trip up even the most seasoned real estate rockstars.

In Chapter 9, I explain why I value continuous improvement, and I tell you which asset I invested $35,616 of my own money in last year... and why.

Finally, in the Appendix you'll find a ***Don't Say "NO" for the Prospect*** toolkit with worksheets, templates and handouts that you can use to create your own success roadmap.

So, sharpen your pencil, grab a highlighter (and a beverage of your choosing), and start reading (er, I mean "engaging")…

We've got this, Rockstars!

Beth

Chapter One

Was I Lucky or Good? My Very First Day in Retail Real Estate

Welcome. What you hold in your hands is a grass roots, no-BS story about how an inexperienced but optimistic sales rookie from the Midwest became a multi-location shopping center owner with more than $79 million in assets. In just a few pages, I'll get into the nitty-gritty of how that happened and what I learned in the process. But first, a short story.

It's the 1980s, and I have just reported for duty at my very first commercial real estate job.

By coincidence (or misfortune), I was the only rookie in the office on that morning. My supervisor sat me in the interns' office, which doubled as the conference room, and tripled as the lunch room.

"Can you get to know this stuff?" She asked me.

"Oh yeah…"

"How fast?"

"FAST!" I was ready!

Mistaking my youthful enthusiasm for confidence, she left…

…for the day.

Forget about being the only intern in the office, now I was the only person in the office.

Uh-oh.

First day of a new job. A bunch of new hire on-boarding papers sitting in a messy pile on the said conference/intern/lunchroom table.

Me, all dressed up, ready to be a rockstar in retail real estate, and utterly, hopelessly clueless. (Folks, I couldn't have told you which was the W4 and which was the WD40 near the window!)

I was ALL enthusiasm. ZERO experience.

I had no idea where to begin or what to do for the day.

Now keep in mind, I couldn't "phone a friend". No way to call "long distance", and cell phones wouldn't be around for a few more years.

It was the 1980s. I couldn't ask my pal Google. Pre-internet. Actually, pre-computer.

I went through the new hire papers in 10 minutes.

Now what?

What do you do when you don't have any idea what you're supposed to be doing? I guess you do what you know.

What I knew was something that I had learned by watching my dad. When I was 11, my father got his real estate license. For the next three years, I would sit at the kitchen table with him every night as he would pour through the white pages and diligently call on people in desirable neighborhoods asking them if they were interested in selling their home.

(Quick side note for my millennials: the white pages was/is a large, printed book with names, addresses and phone numbers of people in your zip code and surrounding neighborhoods.)

Did he get hung up on? Yup. A lot. Did he call the next number when he did? Yup. Always. Did he, over time, build a profitable business with repeat customers? He sure did.

So I picked up the phone, dialed (yes, it was a rotary) 411 (that's how we used to get contact information) and asked the operator (that used to be a job for a real person giving out phone numbers) for the number of Sir Speedy.

Huh?

Sir Speedy is a printing and marketing company (think Kinkos, before Kinkos became Fedex). It was also the one store that I could think of that had more than one location. I happened to have passed it on my way to work that morning.

Seemed like a good place to start prospecting for commercial real estate.

21

Worst case, if I totally panicked on the call, I could always get a bunch of flyers printed, right?

I'm sure my voice was shaking as I explained to the person who picked up the phone that I represented A LOT of properties in South Florida (note that I said "a lot" because I had absolutely no idea how many properties we had).

Then I said, "I have a lot of space...Are you by chance looking to expand?"

That's all I said...

Then, silence (probably because my mouth was so dry with fear).

I actually shut up, and let the other person respond.

"Actually, we are..."

Me: "Really?"

"Yes, we're looking to build our corporate headquarters in Broward County..."

Me: "I think we can help, why don't we get together tomorrow?"

"Perfect."

"Yes," I thought, "perfect".

Now what?

When the bosses got back to the office later that day, I told them about our meeting. They were pleased... and shocked.

Once I reminded them who I was and why I was in their office, we arranged to take the meeting. I know this will sound far-fetched, but the boss had a conflict and had no choice but to let me take this one on my own.

As it turned out, probably because I didn't know any better, I asked the right questions and avoided inadvertently saying *NO* for Sir Speedy.

I took the meeting. We got the account and we brokered the space for the new Sir Speedy headquarters.

(Fun Fact: The landlord that I did this deal with was the same guy who, 22 years later, sold me the second shopping center I invested in, the Shoppes of Arrowhead in Davie, Florida. Coincidence or Canvassing Karma? You decide.)

From that deal, I went from being the rookie to becoming a Leasing Agent, to a Leasing Director, to Leasing VP, to EVP. Eventually I became the President of Terranova Corporation.

After I left Terranova, I dipped my toe into the ownership pool, and today I own six shopping centers worth $79 million in assets. I am also a passive investor in two other retail deals and one multi-unit family complex.

Oh yeah. As I mentioned earlier, I've also "screwed" up plenty along the way. I have...*how shall I say this*... "given back" one shopping center and two pieces of land, and sold a few other properties.

Which brings me back to why I've written this book in the first place.

I have been fortunate to have had great mentors in my life. While I don't have an Ivy League education, I LIVE to learn.

Frankly, and not to bash my fellow "sales trainers"—the majority of whom are very good—but I get frustrated by many of the typical sales training programs.

You see, making a sale has almost nothing to do with how good of a closer you are or can become. It has everything to do with how well you *"open."*

Yet the majority of sales training materials rush through the parts on prospecting. They're so quick to take you to the meeting, to the negotiation and to the close. They purport to do so to focus on the *perceived* most important part of the sale: the close.

But did you know that you can improve your closing rate by as much as 75% if you learn how to "open" better?

To become a "good closer" you have to become an exceptional prospector and pipeline cultivator.

And yet I have not seen a comprehensive and actionable primer dedicated solely to this part of the sale.

This book is.

(Sidenote: the best one I've found so far is Jeb Blount's Fanatical Prospecting.)

What you will read here is not based on the hypothetical. It does not contain "sales theory." It is NOT a collection of tricks, shortcuts, pitches, or canned responses designed to help you overcome some pre-established list of objections so you can easily turn any no to a yes in any situation.

If you want someone who can spoon feed you shortcuts to building lasting and income-producing relationships, I'm sorry, I'm not that person.

If you are looking for the ONE ingredient missing from your secret sauce to success, I suggest you ask your friend Google, 'cause I don't have that either.

What I do have are my own stories and meticulous field notes. I hope that they have captured the steps and strategies I have implemented to maximize my opportunities, compensate for my shortcomings, and manage my mistakes.

More importantly, by organizing my experiences here, I have endeavored to communicate all that I have learned in a way that is both relatable and actionable.

I truly hope that you won't just flip through the chapters, nod in agreement with some of my ideas, maybe laugh at my mistakes and then just put it down and get on with your life. My wish is that you'll use what you've learned to create your own roadmap to success.

Which actually brings me full circle and back to the point of my first story.

What if I had waited for my bosses to come back to the office instead of taking action?

What if I hadn't asked whether Sir Speedy was growing?

What if instead of my mouth drying up, my nerves had caused me to suffer an acute case of verbal diarrhea and I didn't pause my filibuster long enough to hear Sir Speedy's reply?

I'll tell you what would have happened... nothing.

NOTHING WOULD HAVE HAPPENED.

OK, let's pause here... I don't want to give you the wrong impression. Like, for example, that my father blessed me with special genetic sales DNA or that I am just THAT GOOD (or lucky).

Spoiler alert, I'M NOT THAT GOOD (see also Chapter 2), and more importantly, in that moment and for many years thereafter, I had no idea what I had done that had worked. Or why it had worked so quickly.

And thus I had no way of replicating that success.

Today I know what I did.

Do you?

Can you see how this story might offer a clue as to why I've called this book "***Don't Say 'NO' for the Prospect***"?

It's because I didn't say *NO* for the prospect—I didn't say *NO* for Sir Speedy. I called them, even though 99% of "veteran"

26

agents reading this right now would have told me that I was wasting my time.

But I didn't know any better. I didn't know what else I could do that morning, so I called a store that I had passed on my way to work and asked them a simple question. To which, they answered yes.

And look at what happened as a result.

How about you?

How many prospective stores are you passing on your route? Exactly how many have you called?

The reality is that we all have this type of income-limiting *"NO"* conversation continuously and silently running in the background of our minds.

It can prevent us from acting. It can needlessly limit our opportunities. And, I bet you don't even realize that you're having this inner dialogue, or notice all the ways in which it has you saying **"'NO' for Your Prospects"**.

But after you've read this book, you will.

More importantly, you'll see how easy it is to avoid doing this and how quickly your pipeline of prospects will grow as a result.

In the following pages, I'll be sharing my real-life stories, what I did that has kept me from saying *"NO"* for my prospects for years, what's worked and what flat out didn't.

You'll get the honest post-game analysis from me *without the spin*. Most importantly, you'll be able to identify exactly how to benefit from my experience.

One final and critical note from our story: my results (and yours) reflect not what we know, but what we do with that knowledge.

Whether you're already a retail real estate superstar ready to buy your first shopping center, just starting out on the path to retail real estate rockstar, or somewhere in between, you will find lessons in my stories that you can implement right away.

I want you to do so because I want you to succeed!

After you've read the book, if you have questions about how to use what you've learned in your own life, please feel free to contact me. Don't forget to check out the reader-exclusive downloads, tools, print-outs, and leasing agent resources available at **www.DontSayNoForTheProspect.com**.

Reader-Exclusive Downloads

As a complement to this book, check out my website, **DontSayNoForTheProspect.com**. There you'll have instant access to exclusive and premium content including video-based "how to" tutorials, additional articles, audio recordings, downloadable templates, links to the books that I read, and important industry resources that I use every day in my own business and much more.

Lessons Learned

1. To get ahead, you first have to get a head start! The successful people in our business aren't lucky—they're busy. If you'd like to learn more about what they're busy doing and how they're doing it, then keep reading.

I'm often asked whether to cold-call by phone or visit; whether to target canvass or market canvass; whether to follow up with a text or a handwritten note. My answer to all of the above is YES! Of course, there is a preferred approach for each situation (which I try to cover in this book), but I'd much rather you do the less preferred approach, or both, than nothing at all! *Don't Say NO for the Prospect.*

2. To get a good response, you have to first learn to get to the point FAST. Time is a VERY precious commodity. Guard your own time and respect your prospect's time by being direct.

3. To quote sales training legend Tom Hopkins, "Tellin' isn't Sellin'; Asking is!" The whole point of meeting someone for the first time is to open a dialogue. Here's a novel idea. Want to get someone talking to you? **Ask them a question!**

4. And then, let them answer! A good dialogue is a two-way dialogue. When someone is speaking, focus on what they're saying and NOT on what you want to say when they stop. My Dad used to say that God gave us two ears and just one mouth for a good reason! If you're listening twice as much as you're talking in your meetings, then you are going to be successful.

Chapter Two

How One Phone Call with a South Florida Icon *Should* Have Changed the Trajectory of My Career... But Didn't

Wayne Huizenga was/is a South Florida icon (RIP, Mr. Huizenga).

He led Waste Management. He founded Blockbuster Video. He started AutoNation. He owned the Miami Dolphins, He brought hockey to South Florida with the Florida Panthers, and he owned the Miami Marlins (when they were good).

He also taught me the most important lesson in my career. He's why I *"don't say 'NO' for the prospect."*

WE CAN ALL LEARN FROM MY MISTAKE.

So here goes...

31

I was about one year into this real estate thing. I had 17 shopping centers in my leasing portfolio, one of which was an 18,000 "L"-shaped, completely vacant center with blocked visibility in Lake Worth, Florida.

Lake Worth, for those who may not know, is not exactly a booming metropolis, especially 30 years ago. The entire center was vacant except for a bar called the Thirsty Camel.

I'll tell you, I was feeling pretty darn good about myself when the phone rang that morning.

I made a little face (*C'mon, I was busy*) and answered, "This is Beth Azor."

At first all that I heard was static.

And then a voice said, "'Hey—can you hear me…'

I said: 'Barely…'

Then he said: 'Oh I'm sorry, I'm on a cell phone..'

Well, that should have been my first clue. At the risk of showing my, ahem, 'experience', back then only the most powerful and successful people had a cell phone.

But no.

Oh the arrogance. ;)

So, Lesson 1: Don't be arrogant—no matter how accomplished you are. Ever notice how the more accomplished someone is, the less arrogant they seem to act. Whether you are leasing your first center or you own 17, take the extra minute to find out who is on the other end of that call!

I wish I had.

"I'm interested in leasing your 6,000 square foot end cap in Lake Worth," he continued.

"Sure, what kind of business are you in?"

"I want to open a video store."

"Ha!"

(Yes, I said, "Ha!"—out loud. *Oh, the arrogance.*)

Then I gathered myself.

"A video store? Sir, the space is 6,000 square feet. What could you possibly do with all of that space?"

Then he said the one sentence that anyone who has been in the leasing business has heard 1,000 times.

"Oh, I'm starting a new company and this is going to be my prototype store and then we're going to franchise…"

"Oh sir…," I sighed. "… I'm sure that you are going to do all that, but my boss has told me that this space is already built out for a restaurant, and I have to lease it to a restaurant."

He replied, "That's too bad. I really like the location. The visibility, exposure to the highway, and ingress/egress is perfect.

Why don't you take my name and my cell phone number (again the cell phone) in case your boss changes his mind?"

Contact management was different in those days. Instead of a mobile CRM system, we had prospect sheets that we would fill out by hand and then file in an accordion file that was organized by months. The more important the prospect, the earlier we would file it in the calendar for follow up.

After taking down Mr. Huizenga's information (by the way, I butchered the spelling of his name since I didn't even bother to ask for clarification), I filed this prospect sheet one year out. No need to rush with this guy.

That's not all. I actually wrote a note on the sheet: "Video Store—6,000 Square Feet—Ha!" (I really wish I still had that sheet. It would be framed and hung in my office!)

I was so arrogant —don't be arrogant.

Meanwhile, one year later...

Blockbuster Video had opened in 40 locations and would eventually grow into a publicly-traded Fortune 500 company that at its peak employed 84,000 people in 9,000 stores. Oops. My arrogance had caused me to silently say 'NO' to Mr. Huizenga, without even giving him a chance. Who lost here? Uh, *me*! If only I had asked him the right questions!

Years later I met Mr. Huizenga again. He was the keynote speaker at a conference that I was chairing. He thought my story was so hilarious that he shared it with the 3,000 conference attendees during his speech.

Which was OK with me because I am a teacher. There's a lot to learn from this one.

Such as...

When my phone rang, I needed to do one thing... *just one thing!*

After Mr. Huizenga had told me his plans, I needed to ask one question, "Well sir, what do you do now?"

Think about what could have happened if I had been *interested* instead of *arrogant*?

He would have said, "Oh, I run Waste Management..."

I would have shown him the space, and maybe 8,999 more.

But, I didn't ask. **I said "NO" for him.**

Did I mention that I was arrogant? *Don't be arrogant.*

Arrogance closes more doors than it opens. Stay humble.
TONI PAYNE

No matter how successful you are, never forget that you can learn from everyone you meet. Why not take one extra minute to ask them a few appropriate questions?

Worried that the questions may seem a little intrusive to a prospect on the first "date"?

Here's a tip: start by saying something light, like: "I'm new (or I'm in a Reality Show) and my boss/producer makes me ask these questions. Sorry, but any help you can give me will make a good impression and be very much appreciated…"

Worst case scenario, you learn nothing new. Best case… well…everyone starts with one location. Some expand.

Even if you don't get through every question on the call-in sheet, from now on, commit to asking ask every single prospect these two magic questions!

1. **What do you do now?**

2. **What caused you to call on my center today?**
(Translation: what did you like about my center that made you pick up the phone/drop by today?)

That's how I always start now when meeting a start-up for the first time. With these two questions, you will be able to learn enough about your prospect to see if s/he's a good fit for your product/service/space or for someone else's.

Here you'll see the call-in sheet that I use for each and every prospect call. The more questions that you can answer on it, the easier it will be for you (and your bosses) to determine if you've got a real prospect or a time-waster. In my office, we make it a weekly contest; whoever has filled in the most answers on their sheets for the week, wins the commission! Just kidding, they win a gift card (the commission comes later).

30 More Qualifying Questions to Ask Prospects
BEFORE YOU GIVE THE RENTAL RATES

Name: _____ Phone #: _____

Email address: _____

Type of business: _____ SF needed: ___ Inline/OP/endcap: _____

Own Business Now: ___ If yes, how many years? __ Where: _____

What do you like about your current location?

_____

What don't you like about your current location?

_____

More than one location? ___

If yes, what makes you successful? _____

Current revenues: ____ If no, have you completed a business plan?___

Projected first year revenues:

_____

*** What do you like about our center?

_____

Start-up capital needed: _____ Any Partners? _____

How much capital do you have? _____ Who will sign Lease? _____

Rent budget: _____ Funding sources: _____

Have you researched the area?

_____

Why do you like the area?

_____

What other areas/centers have you looked at? _____

_____

Sign needs: _____ Parking needs: _____

Tough Stuff: A Personal Guarantee is required.

Other issues that may pose as objections down the line:

_____

If they ask you for the rate, simply let them know that you'll be happy to *give* it to them. You just want to be sure that you understand exactly what they're looking for... and that you have something that can suit their needs.

Then say, "I still have a couple of quick questions..."

If you can get all or most of these questions answered on the first call, not only will you avoid saying *"NO"* for a huge prospect, but also your job is 95% done. Your improved time management alone will boost your income by 30%!

(Sidenote: Notice that when I'm discussing the concept of rates, I say "give," instead of "quote" or "ask." "Give" conjures images of gifts and stirs feelings of joy; you don't negotiate a "gift." "Quote" and "ask", on the other hand, scream that you're negotiable! Ugh!!)

Chapter Three

The *"NO"* Habit: Are You Silently Saying *NO* to Yourself to Avoid Hearing Someone Else Say It to You?

Are you silently saying no to yourself?

If so, stop doing that.

Actually, it's not your fault.

In fact, you may not even realize you're doing it, but we all silently say *"NO for the prospect"* (and for others) all the time.

"NO, they won't be interested."

"NO, they're just a one-store wonder."

"NO, they're not growing."

"NO, they can't afford our rates."

These phrases and similar objections pop up in our minds reflexively. We don't consciously conjure them. Frankly, we don't even actively hear them... but unfortunately we do listen to them.

Why is that?

Not to get too deep, but I think it's because we're conditioned from birth to equate saying "no" with power; and hearing the word "no" with shame and helplessness.

Grown-ups say no...

"No, you can't touch that."

"No, you won't go there."

"No, you don't eat those."

As kids, we're often told that we have to learn to "accept no for an answer..."

You've probably heard "no" a lot in your life. I have. And I'm betting you didn't like it much. I didn't.

What's more, I'm guessing that on at least one occasion you did everything you could to avoid hearing another "no". I know I sure did.

So what's my point?

As adults, we still do whatever we can to avoid hearing no, often subconsciously, by saying no in our minds on behalf of someone *before* we ask him/her even a single question.

We also avoid hearing no *consciously*. We do this by asking only those questions we expect our prospect(s) to say yes to (hello, *Spin Selling*).

This is to our own detriment.

It gets worse.

When as adults we hear "no" from someone else, we automatically revert to our powerless child selves and rebel with a reflexive and power affirming, "I will NOT take 'no' for an answer."

Ever clicked on a random nutrition supplement ad or hung out with someone who just became an independent distributor for [insert favorite weight loss solution here]?

Hide your wallet!

"C'mon Beth, it's just one sample order... you can cancel anytime... (after of course my commission check comes in). I simply won't take no for an answer..."

How's that arm-twisting tactic working out... We all know (and RUN FROM) that person, right?

Folks, it's time to grow up. It's time to interrupt the endless loop of "no" playing as background noise in our head. It simply doesn't make adult sense. It is counterproductive either to be so averse to hearing "no" from someone else that you reflexively say it for them first--or to be so shamed and offended by every "no" that you do hear that you feel compelled to wrestle it into a "yes."

It's bad for your soul and for your business.

Reader Challenge

Do you know how many times you are inadvertently saying "NO" for a particular prospect?

Stop reading now and spend the next 12 hours counting and recording the number of times you catch yourself wanting to or actually saying *NO* for a prospect. Seriously, put down this book for half a day and take stock of the silent "NO's" in the soundtrack of your mind. Try to catch the times your boss or a real estate vet says, "NO" FOR you—as in, "Don't waste your time." Write everything down on the page below and shoot me an email, take a screenshot or message me with what you learned when you're finished.

---

10 Ways We Saying "NO" For Someone Else!

We may be saying *"NO"* when:

- We don't get out there and meet enough (or any) new people who can say "no" to us. (*Hello, people are prospects!*) Are you going to network events? How often?

    Do you meet new people at the events or do you "hang" with people you already know?

    Here's a tip: go up to the person standing alone. There's always someone standing alone. He or she will *love* you for saving them! Don't like large groups? Call a few real estate peers and host your own smaller gathering.

- We don't get to our (or any) point quickly. (Time is money.)

- We don't ask the right (or any) question(s).

- Our fear (of rejection) says "no" for us.

- We don't shut up long enough to allow someone to answer our questions.

    Hey, this means you, Mr./Ms. Sales Person! You know that you're just waiting for me to stop talking so you can make your point—which is the very definition of "listening" from a sales person's point of view!

10 Ways We Saying "NO" for Someone Else! (continued)

- We're not willing to take any chances or make any mistakes (We grow more from our failures than from our successes.)

- We don't know why we have succeeded (or failed), so we can't replicate our success or learn from our mistakes.

- We learn, but we don't apply what we've learned from our successes (and failures) in our next actions.

- We're arrogant and/or dismissive (as in we laugh out loud at an icon, OR we assume the front-desk clerk is NOT the owner).

- We don't recognize or refuse to accept a legitimate "no," and thus miss out on building a potentially fruitful relationship.

You'll find this in the Appendix as well, so that you can print it and post it near your workstation.

I bet you can think of a dozen more ways we say *"NO"* For Our Prospects… Feel free to add and tag your own to my list at **#DontSayNo**.

Now that we understand the habit of saying "NO," let's take a look at how this silently plays out in our day-to-day lives.

Chapter Four

The One Thing That 97% of Leasing Agents Do When They Meet a Prospect That You Should NEVER Do... And What to Do Instead

I love to canvass (prospect door-to-door or store-to-store) with my clients, and I have gone canvassing with hundreds, maybe thousands of leasing agents.

Want to guess the first question most agents ask (even seasoned ones) when they walk into a retail store?

"Is the owner here?"

Now when you ask that person at the cash register if the owner is there, what that person actually hears is, **"Is there someone way more important than you here?"**

But, Beth? I need to get to the decision maker.

Yes, I know that you've been told umpteen times to "only speak to the decision maker!" I know that there are legions of books dedicated to getting around the "gatekeeper."

However, this question is just lose-lose.

Think about it. What if they *are* the owner (or his/her spouse)?

You think they'll be flattered?

Um, no. What is he or she going to say in response? And more importantly: How is he or she going to feel?

He or she is going to think "Who is this person, and why wouldn't they think I'm in charge?"

S/he's NOT going to feel honored and respected.

And what if the person is *not* the owner?

They feel the same disrespect. They'll think to themselves, "You think I'm not good enough to own this place?"

I think we can all agree that respect is very important in cultivating a relationship. That's what you're doing when canvassing: planting seeds to grow what you hope will be a fruitful relationship, or trying to.

(Remember, if you offend the people you want to befriend, ***you just said "NO" for them.****)*

You know there's a time-honored question oft asked of executives during corporate retreats: Would you rather be liked or respected?

In sales, it's important to be both. If they don't like you and they don't respect you, they won't buy from you. According to a recent study by Harvard Business School, 90% of consumers say that they bought something because they liked the person who was selling it to them.

Not only does this opening question make the prospect feel disrespected, **it makes them dislike you for asking it**.

When you're canvassing, your only goal is to open a dialogue with a potential prospect. Unfortunately that's very difficult to do when your opener is a non-starter that offends the person you're trying to get to know.

By the way, this applies even if (perhaps especially if) the cashier is 12 years old. They may not be the owner today, but you can bet their parents are and that they hope that someday they will be.

So I suggest an alternate approach, one that embraces everyone as a potential prospect and doesn't put you at risk to accidentally say *"NO"* for someone. (Like the person working the cash register who may actually be able to help you meet your goals.)

First, when you walk into a new establishment DO NOT walk around the store pretending to be a shopper or start buttering up the clerk by effusively praising the merchandise. Ugh. That's just gross and obvious.

Instead, when you enter, greet whomever you meet politely and launch right into your purpose for being there! People are busy. You demonstrate respect for someone by respecting their time. Get right to the point.

"Hey, I have a shopping center a few miles away. What are your expansion plans?"

Then, if/when they reply, you can begin establishing a rapport. Instead of inconsequential and inauthentic "schmoozing," you will have made the prospect feel valued by a) respecting their valuable time; b) listening to their responses; and c) asking for additional input and opinion.

Your goal is simply to find out:

1. if your prospect has a need, and

2. if you can help them with that need.

You create an authentic rapport and lay the foundation for a relationship by concentrating on what your prospect is saying. Listen without interrupting and without formulating your next question while they're still speaking.

(Tom Hopkins calls this flawed method "Showing Up & Throwing Up." Don't do it!)

If you do learn to listen, what you'll soon find is that most retail mom & pops opened their first store with the American dream to open more! Most will be thrilled to tell you all about it. What's more, I've found that most are extremely interested in commercial real estate. So let them know right away that you're in the real estate business.

Trust me, they think about it and like to discuss real estate. And, now you're talking your language. Now you're building a real and substantive rapport. You're demonstrating your value and you're planting a seed as to how you will be the person who can help them achieve their expansion dreams.

This is how I got to know the owner of my favorite ice-cream store and eventually got him to move from his "A" space to my "B" space. (Quick tip: want to impress a prospect with your market knowledge? You might want to read Chapter 7 first).

Incidentally, the "gatekeepers" like talking about real estate too. Ask the gatekeeper if they know your center. If they do, ask them what ideas they have for new uses needed in the market! The gatekeeper holds a lot of weight with the owners. Treat them accordingly—with respect!

If you edit out, *"Are you the owner?"* from your "pitch," you

Bonus Resource

Sign my Prospecting Pledge in the Appendix to join the top 2%.

will get the owner's name and contact information (at a minimum) 90% of the time! I promise!

This is only one example of how a small adjustment in your approach to the prospecting process can have a dramatic impact on your end results.

There are many others, but perhaps none is more important than making a commitment to consistently canvass (prospect) in the first place.

Chapter Five

Why I Focus on Something That 98% of Retail Leasing Agents Overlook

Here's a pop quiz that I give to my rock stars at the start of each class... Let's take it now.

Question 1. How many vacant spaces do you have?

Question 2. How many call-ins do you get each week?

Question 3. How many of those are *qualified*?

Note that in my world, a store is qualified IF (and only IF) they meet these two benchmarks:

1. They have more than one location (the more the better —I get goosebumps when I hear 3 locations!)

2. They have money on-hand! Are they planning to invest or is a partner perhaps funding the expansion? What are their year-to-date (YTD) sales? Use the questions on the call-in sheet that we reviewed in the previous chapter to find out. Remember, having sales in more than one location means they are paying rent, and can likely continue to do so!

Want to guess how many calls a week typically fit my definition of qualified calls?

.05%

So, my last question: If you have so many [insert your number here] spaces to fill, and only a small number of leads coming in off the leasing sign, and only .05% of those calls are actually qualified, how are you going to fill your spaces?

Um… perhaps you should consider canvassing.

Yet only 2% of all agents say that they regularly canvass.

My guess is that it's the top 2%.

Because…

… If there is one thing that all successful shopping centers and leasing agents have in common it's that they all curate and cultivate relationships all the time.

How do they do it?

Well, they cold call. But they also canvass (get out of their office and prospect door-to-door).

I canvass.

Actually everyone on my team canvasses. 10 hours per week minimum.

Here's why…

… *it works.*

In today's tech-obsessed, information-saturated, and distracted world, it's no longer who you know, it's **who knows YOU!** (Credit: Michelle Villalobos and Dale Scott)

With the sheer volume of *stuff* at everyone's disposal, you don't want to be a "stealth" salesperson, lost in someone's in-box.

If you plan to break through this noise, you're going to have to get out there, meet and actually talk to people face-to-face.

I heard this from an admissions rep on a college tour with my son. She said, "When we 'know' you, it's harder for us to say 'No' to you." It's true. Conversely, if your prospects don't feel like they know you, how can you expect them to do business with you?

Face-to-face canvassing is FAR more effective for identifying qualified mom and pops than cold calling or sending broadcast emails from a list ever could be.

In fact, I routinely average 15 new business cards for every 15 stores I visit. It's true, and I've been in my market for 31 years. Yes, as shocking as it is, I wind up learning something new, finding new prospects and uses each time I hit the street.

Often, there's something right in front of me that I'd been missing for years.

I'll give you a quick example (though I could give you 10). Last month I was out and about doing some market canvassing with two of my rookies.

(Side note: market canvassing, as opposed to target canvassing, is when you go store-to-store-to-store within a specific geographic area. Target canvassing, on the other hand, is when you contact/visit stores with one particular use, e.g., wedding dress/formal wear shops, bike stores, etc.)

There's a tennis shop on my route to my son's school that I had probably passed for two straight years. I'd been meaning to stop in, but they looked small and I figured they were a one-shop situation.

It took my newbies to remind me that I was saying *"NO"* for the prospect. Sufficiently chastened, we went in. Yeah... you guessed it.

They had 8 locations, and were looking for more. Crazy!

Sometimes even a grizzled old(ish) retail leasing vet and teacher needs to be reminded to do the basics. We all do. So, to kick start your prospecting effort, here is an example of a Canvassing Plan that I got from DLC Management (Thanks, Christopher Ressa). I now use with all of my clients.

Sample Canvassing Plan

Plan
- We are spending the day canvassing Middletown, NY and Kingston, NY

Goal
- Speak to 50–65 tenants (Big number, high hopes for us)
- Bring in 5–10 small shop leads

Expectations
- Positive attitude all day.
- Be energetic.
- You guys need to review and be familiar with the site plan and the rents. We are focusing on the small shop #105/#107 and #120/#121.
- I have attached the rent table, please have an idea what the gross rents are for each of those spaces.
- I'm not expecting you guys to be pros, just focus on getting better and better after each conversation.

Materials
- 100 colored flyers
- Rent roll

Dress code
- Look good, feel good
- Business casual (Jeans w/ polo or button up)

Times
- Let's plan to leave around 8:45–8:50
- I want to be in Middletown by 9:45
- We will leave and head home once we hit our number

Get Pumped!!!

Oh and there's one more thing. You'll have a lot more success if you do these things.

Before you go canvassing:

1. Complete the "Top 5 Uses" form in the Appendix. When you do, pick a particular center and try to match uses to the square footage that you have available. Be as specific as you possibly can, and consider the following:

- Retail in the surrounding area, especially those uses that produce strong revenue

- any 2nd Generation opportunities you may have (include former restaurant spaces, salon spaces and medical facilities with valuable infrastructure)

- where in the center the vacancies are

- whether the vacant space is better for destination (elbows) or impulse (end caps and good visibility) retailers

- consumer demographics

- exclusives and restrictions (e.g., I can't have pool supply companies in one of my centers because the city prohibits the storage of chlorine)

2. Tell everyone who will listen what you're looking for! I found and leased space to the best burger joint just from a casual conversation that I had with a friend. A week after we had

spoken, my friend texted me while in the middle of eating a burger from this fabulous little spot about 15   miles from my center. In fact, some of my best leads have come from my friends, my kids' friends, parents, and random people I meet. Your vacancies are not trade secrets (unless you're under some sort of non-disclosure, then they are).

3. Make flyers (see also #7).

4. Phone a friend. Go with a colleague, someone from your office or even with a competitor. Canvassing is WAY more fun in pairs, and it should be FUN! Canvassing with a colleague also keeps you accountable. If you set up a date with a peer (especially if that peer is a competitor), I doubt you'll cancel... at least I know you'll think twice before you do.

5. Use Yelp for a little reconnaissance. It's great for picking canvassing destinations for next generation restaurant space, salons, nail salons, etc. That said, don't worry about prior planning. It's more important to just get out there and do it!

When you get there...

6. When you're canvassing, get the owner's business card (yes, I know that's obvious); but now turn it over. More often than not, if a store has multiple locations, the other store addresses will be listed on the back of the business card.

Ideally, you're going to try to get said business card (and turn it over) before you speak to the owner, perhaps while they're engaged with another customer. The reason is that the number of store locations will affect how you speak to the owner. Obviously if you're talking with someone about the 9th location it's a very different discussion than with someone who's just considering their second. Going from 1 to 2 spaces is hard; 2–3 is easier, and once they have 4, they're in the real estate business like you are.

7. BRING the right flyers. If, for example, you have multiple spaces/centers, create at least one flyer that SHOWS (not just lists) all of your centers—perhaps with a map!

If you have a built-out 2nd generation space (like a restaurant or hair salon) and you're target canvassing for that particular use, your fliers should have PICTURES OF THE BUILT OUT SPACE and a list of the important stats on that space. For example, a flyer for a restaurant space should include the size of the grease trap, size of the hood, AC tonnage, electrical amps, etc.

Oh, last thing on flyers: don't forget to give them to whomever you meet while you're still talking to them. Don't hold onto them like they're some top secret document that only a select few have clearance to see.

If, for some reason, the store is closed (and door locked), take a Sharpie pen (always have one with you). I prefer red, but any bright color will do. Write a personal note on your flyer and slip it under the door.

Finally...

8. Get Lost! This one is so important that it warranted a rant (I mean "story").

A few years ago I came across an interesting story in—of all places—Travel & Leisure Magazine. It's title, "Let's Get Lost," caught my eye. The article chronicled a couple who accidentally typed "Carpi" for "Capri" into their navigation system and four hours later were shocked to find themselves in a landlocked city instead of the island destination they had intended to visit. Interestingly, the pair never noticed that on their journey they had neither crossed over water, nor even seen a bridge... usual telltale signs that you're headed to an island, right?

Though the author was writing a tongue in cheek piece as a tech insider, the deeper meaning was clear: While technology may have made getting lost obsolete, we are clearly very "misguided."

Not to get on a soap box (or risk alienating my millennials), I couldn't agree more. Normally I wouldn't waste your time on a personal pet peeve... but I consider this particular tip a professional imperative.

I know that many of you believe that a GPS system is the must-have tool for all leasing agents. Most of the time I agree. But sometimes, they are a mere distraction; and at worst, they are inhibiting our natural navigational instincts to the point that we are missing opportunities at every turn—literally.

Truth is, there are prospecting opportunities for you on every corner. Maybe even your own.

I found Caneswear, an iconic destination University of Miami apparel warehouse because I noticed that as football season got underway, their lawn signs would pop up on the median of the road in front of one of my shopping centers. I figured that if they were looking for exposure on my street, I should offer it to them. So I did.

Two years later they left their warehouse for my retail space, and their sales have literally quintupled. They have lines out the door and have already expanded!

All because a) I had my eyes open and b) I didn't say *"NO"* for a *warehouse* prospect.

Although they're on the wrong team (go 'Noles), in this case, everybody won!

Remember, everywhere you turn you will find someone or something that presents you with an untapped resource or opportunity. But you can't leverage what you don't see.

Any tool, device or "GPS system" that prevents you from interacting with your surroundings should at least be occasionally discarded. Period. Exclamation point!

Your Top Canvassing Questions Answered

Why Don't Leasing Agents Canvass?
I don't know, but here are my best guesses (in no particular order): pride, fear of rejection, laziness, too busy doing something else (time management is in the next book). What do you think keeps people (I mean, you) from getting out there?

When Should I Canvass?
Every week, but it depends on your needs/goals/metrics (you can fill out the canvassing worksheet in the Appendix to create a personalized plan). I canvass every Tuesday afternoon from 1–4pm (30 business cards or 3 hours, whichever comes first). When I was a rookie, I canvassed every day. My goal was to meet 50–100 prospects every single day.

How Can I Make Canvassing Easier?
Canvass with a peer, a friend, family member or a competitor; it'll be more fun. I go with my boys; it's a blast. When you canvass with a peer or competitor, you'll get additional intel AND you'll have an accountability partner (kind of like having a gym buddy).

What Should Be My Goal from Canvassing?
The only canvassing goal is dialogue (and a business card). Do NOT expect to "close" any deals on a canvassing trip.

What Should I Take with Me When I Canvass?
When you canvass, bring a flyer that has:
- All of the centers you have (WITH A MAP)—when you can, give your prospects a choice
- Pictures of your 2nd generation space (i.e., turnkey restaurant, turnkey hair salon) with as much specific information as possible
- Pictures/logos nearby tenants
- Local demos

Bonus Benefit to Canvassing

There's another far less-known benefit to consistent canvassing.

Each time you return from a canvassing expedition, you will experience the magic of canvassing karma.

You know that edge of your seat, slightly nauseous feeling you get while waiting for the phone to ring with good news? Well, go canvassing! When you return, you will have good news waiting for you!

Although I have no scientific data on the magic of canvassing karma, I do have personal experience, not to mention a boatload of anecdotal evidence and emails from students that confirm its existence. Next time that you find yourself in that ambiguous waiting position, hit the street—do a little prospecting. I promise when you get back, you'll have good news waiting.

Do you still need more reasons to canvass?

Here's another: find new uses for retail spaces that you wouldn't think of. For example, in one day, in one center, I found three new uses I had NEVER heard of or previously considered:

• A wig store for cancer patients that would be a perfect match for 2nd generation salon sites

- A portrait studio that was in a deceptively large 10,000 square foot elbow space that would be great for any large destination space

- A public school lunch provider (caterers) for 2nd generation restaurant sites that no one wants

Chapter Six

Beyond Canvassing: Other Prospecting Strategies That Work (If You Work Them the Right Way)

My old school reputation being what it is (see previous chapter), I'm often asked if I believe that there are any worthy prospecting strategies beyond canvassing.

"Beyond canvassing?!" Blasphemy!

OK, I admit it… I may have been a little late to the social media scene, but now I'm now officially all in, especially on Facebook. In the past eighteen months, I (as well as many of my agents, interns and clients) have been getting an incredible 32% response rate when direct messaging mom and pop retailers.

I also started testing the impact of texting a prospect right after a call with them (and I mean right after). So far, the results are EXCELLENT! (A whopping 40% increase in setting showing appointments!)

Bonus Tip: I learned that even today, very few mom/pops have professional email addresses. They all, however, have cell phones. Use them.

For national and regional retailers, LinkedIn is increasingly effective as a way to break through the email spam cycle. It's merely supply and demand for attention. When a national retailer steps away from their desk, they often return to 300 new emails. Hard to get noticed in that kind of volume. LinkedIn, on the other hand, is still less trafficked and most retailers have LinkedIn alerts and notifications on their devices.

I've found that national retailers simply respond faster on LinkedIn, and I use it as a great way both to stay on top of new openings and to get appointments with them at Shopping Center Conferences.

And you can still "cold call" Nationals, but only AFTER you've already sent them (and confirmed that they've received) detailed information about your center, their locations in your market, along with their competitors' locations...and how you can help them with their needs.

Use Yelp when sourcing restaurants; you may want to avoid anything with less than 3 stars.

You can still use email blasts to reach your best market, the tenant rep brokers. DO NOT, however, use a list-generated email blast when reaching out to national retailers. They hate getting massive and impersonal emails. You and your email will go right to their Spam folder. Also, if you're targeting restaurants, make sure to create a separate restaurant-specific tenant rep list.

You should also be regularly skimming the advertisements and "advertorials" in local print magazines and industry dailies.

Another thing, I bet you also get leads sent directly to your home! Don't laugh at me. **DON'T SAY NO FOR THE PROSPECT!!!**

All households get bulk-mail—you know those "valpaks" full of coupons from local retailers? Don't just toss that direct mail packet. It's a treasure trove of retail riches! I guarantee you that at least one of those retailers is worth a cold call.

Remember, if they can afford to advertise, they have sales. Sales means they can afford rent!

Also, small and neighborly networking groups, like your local Chamber, can be a great resource for identifying what's happening in your center's/client's market... and for getting leads. Join them. Make sure that you show up and actually participate.

(Remember the college admissions rep I mentioned in Chapter 5. She said, "When we 'know' you, it's harder for us to say 'No' to you.")

If you are an active member of your local Chamber, for example, you'll likely become the go-to commercial real estate expert for other active members. Now consider this: On average there are 300 members in every local Chamber. Ten percent of Chamber members own stores and pay rent... that's thirty real prospects right off the bat.

Finally, a word on the #1 question I get from leasing agents around the country:

"Beth, how do I get national retailers to respond to me?!"

It's a complicated question with simple, but not easy, answers. It takes effort—and individualization. You can't mass-market to retailers; you have to cast a narrow and focused net. Ideally you are personalizing all of your communications with nationals so your message matches their market and needs. So, when targeting nationals, pick ten that you want to target. Then, go one-by-one and follow these guidelines.

How to Target National Retailers

DO YOUR RESEARCH. Make sure their current location is not adjacent or across the street from your site. Or if it is, be upfront about it and tell them why you're reaching out (e.g., Can you add a drive-thru for them?). Don't bother targeting a company that you know is not already in or expanding to your market.

Alternatively, you can specifically state that you know that they aren't in your market *yet*, but you're inquiring as to when they may be coming. By the way, this information is readily available—it's worth a Google search, don't you think?

INCLUDE THE ADDRESS AND CITY OF YOUR SITE. Folks, I can't tell you how many times I have heard that this information is omitted. Focus on the "Big Rocks," the most important items first. I'd say that including where you are is a BOULDER! Don't leave your address off of your correspondence.

KNOW THE DEMOS THAT ARE MOST IMPORTANT TO THEM; DO NOT INCLUDE GENERAL DEMOS. See the next chapter (7) on the importance of doing a proper Market Study before you do anything else. Be as specific in your data points as you can. If you know they like college grads, or are looking for a market with a particular percentage of children, include that with your initial email.

Research and provide demos that pertain to the retailer. **Yes, it's more work, but you want to know how they will respond faster, right?** Also, some retailers like Pet Supermarket, for example, now want to know the coordinates of the site so they can input the address on their geo system. In fact, give them all a map and coordinates (see Ninja tip at the end of this box)!

SHOW THEM YOUR CREATIVITY & YOUR INTEGRITY. If you are thinking about them possibly relocating or expanding from a nearby store, tell them you KNOW they are adjacent or across the street. Don't let them think you are being lazy!

FOLLOW UP! FOLLOW UP! FOLLOW UP! This is the retailers' #1 complaint: leasing agents do not follow up. Timing is everything (see Chapter 8). Things change. Just because they gave you a "NO" three months ago, don't automatically SAY NO FOR THEM—it could be a yes this time. (I went to ask Costco to lease a former Kmart. It happened on the 15th time when I flew to their headquarters.) It might take 10–15 "Not Right Now No's" before the time is right. So be patient and FOLLOW UP!

Also, be proactive in how you follow up. Do your research. There are no excuses to not be informed. You no longer have to cull your own news or rely on outdated accordion files to ping your memory.

We have this new fangled thing called Google Alerts (I hear it's gonna be big). Use it. Enter the retailer's name and key words about their store and you will be the first to learn about their latest plans. You can use this intel as a reason to re-initiate a conversation.

Now, as we've discussed, it can be inappropriate and counterproductive to NEVER TAKE NO FOR AN ANSWER. If a store gives you a valid reason for not being interested in your space or services, thank them for their feedback and move on. No need to follow up later for one year unless their circumstances change.

That said, when you do hear "no," please ask "why" as in, "why doesn't my site work for you?" That's the only common sense way I've found to easily distinguish between when something is a "Not Right Now" and something is a "Not Ever."

NATIONALS NINJA EXTRA CREDIT TIP #1. Map their competitors. Retailers get approximately 50–100 calls per week. If you send a site and they review it only to find that they have a site across the street, they will less likely look at future sites you send them. You have wasted their time and the retailers have long memories.

However, if you do your homework, and even go the extra mile and map their competitors around your site, they will respond much more quickly. You will be placed in the category of a leasing agent who does NOT waste their time! They will remember that too, and respond to you faster in the future.

Your reputation grows as your career does. It can take years to build a good reputation, but only a minute to lose it.

Retailers who represent smaller chains usually grow into larger box stores. Act as if! The research you do in introducing yourself (and your sites) to them, even if they're not ready for you yet, is an investment in your future in the retail industry. Be smart! Go the extra mile!

NATIONALS NINJA EXTRA CREDIT TIP # 2. Calling on national retailers—and getting them to respond to you—is so challenging that I decided to take the unconventional step of... *wait for it...* asking a bunch of them what exactly would make them feel compelled to respond.

In the Appendix, you'll find an entire section with their answers. There are 17 ways (at least) that you can use to get national retailers to call you back. All of these ways come as direct suggestions from the national retailers themselves. Check them out now!

Chapter Seven

Do Your Homework or Don't Even Bother!

Abe Lincoln is believed to have said that if he had 6 hours to chop down a tree, he'd spend the first 4 sharpening his axe.

I feel that way about filling space and making deals. If you told me I had to close 10 new deals in 10 days, I'd spend 9 days sharpening my strategy.

OK, perhaps I'm embellishing. Maybe spending 9 days to prepare or to gather market intel is a little excessive, but spending 90 minutes (minimum) in those 9 days is not.

There is nothing more fundamental to your ultimate success than having a thorough, up-to-date and accurate understanding of what's happening in your market.

So, do you know what's happening?

- with your own space?

- your competitors' spaces? Are there new entrants in the market? Are they raising/lowering rents?

- your prospects' businesses? Are they growing, fading, being disrupted? How?

- the local market demographics? Are they shifting? How?

- Is there roadwork? Are new companies coming into the market? Are there local universities in the market that are looking to increase enrollment?

You need to be able to answer these questions because a good market study is the foundation of a good leasing strategy and a key building block of long-term success.

This is not exactly a novel idea. In fact, if you do a Google search for "market study," you'll find 465,000,000 responses. That's a LOT of information—too much information!

Clearly finding how to do a market study is simple (like a lot of things we've discussed in this book). Anyone can (and should) be doing them on a regular basis.

But we often don't.

That's partly because we think it's a waste of time... we often just go with *our gut*.

This can work; we can get away without doing a market study... once. Think back to my experience with Sir Speedy (Chapter 1).

But when you have no idea why you were successful at something, it's awfully difficult to replicate.

Without insight, "luck" tends to run out quickly and you're left wondering how to replicate your success. Market intelligence, which gives you real insight and knowledge that you can obtain only through research, is the key to building relationships. Relationships will drive and sustain your business for years.

Market studies come in so many shapes, sizes, and varieties. Nearly every industry has its own version. For example, if you've taken any basic marketing class, you've seen a SWOT Analysis: Strengths, Weaknesses, Opportunities, and Threats. In politics, people do polls and voter behavior analysis. Advertisers do focus groups and consumer studies.

Market intel is the reason why Facebook and Google exist. That's how ubiquitous market data has become, for better or worse. The great part is that with the resources available now, you don't need 9 days to gather it.

Aside from using Google, Facebook, LinkedIn, Twitter, etc., I also recommend:

• Getting out there in person to do your research. There's no law against visiting your competitor's centers.

• Calling and having coffee with neighboring leasing agents to get the real scoop (or host an intimate happy hour). Let's face it, social media has less than perfect information. You should be making friends with your peers and sharing information (and leads, when appropriate). There is no substitute for good, first-person intel.

- Forwarding a lead to a competitor. Why not? If you have a prospect that you can't help, send him/her to a competitor who might be able to. Not only will you build goodwill, but high occupancy in a market increases ALL rents!

I promise you, if you put in the work, you will get the appointment. The retailers grouse all the time that we leasing agents do not do our homework. They say the agents that do the homework get faster responses!

I got a piece of advice from a national retailer with over 150 locations: "Show that you did some tenant-specific advance prep for the meeting." I can assure you that my own experience affirms that to be true. Prepare! Prepare! Prepare!!!

The best part? If you put the time in beforehand, you'll set yourself apart from your competitors and from many of your colleagues.

The Importance of Playing Offense: Setting Goals, Tracking Your Numbers and Making Course Corrections

Like canvassing—and like market research—setting goals and planning to meet those goals is something that everyone knows they should be doing. Yet once again, so many of us never actually get around to doing this.

Why is that?

Would you feel comfortable going on an expensive vacation without knowing important stuff like whether it's warm or cold where you're headed, with whom you're going or how long you'll be gone? I doubt it... I mean, how would you pack? (By the way, if you answered yes, I probably can't help you.)

For everyone else, the most obvious reason to set goals in business and in life is that without knowing where you intended to go you'll never know whether you're off course (until it's too late).

I get calls from agents who aren't doing well that want me to help them improve.

My first question is, "How do you know that you're doing poorly?"

They'll answer with something like:

"My boss." Or...

"I'm not doing enough deals." Or...

"I'm not making enough money."

C'mon peeps, you've got to be able to do better than that!

I was at a conference about a year ago when an associate said something I completely agreed with. He said we are in the business of offense and defense.

Unfortunately, most of us play defense. In other words, we react to life's plays, react to our bosses' plays, or react to our competitors' plays. What we really need is to play OFFENSE!

We need to be creating OUR own plays!

So, I ask more questions, like:

- What's your playbook look like?

- Do you know your budget goal?

- Do you know what numbers you need to target to meet your budget goal?

- What have you been doing to meet your targets?

- Break it down for me... what did you do yesterday? *No seriously, what did you do yesterday?*

- What time did you get up, get to the office?

- How many calls did you receive?

- How many did you make?

- How many times did you show your space?

- How many cards did you collect? How many stores did you canvass? (Canvassing is part of playing offense.)

You should be able to answer all of these questions because you should be taking 15 minutes per day, at a minimum, to work on offense. This is time for you to set and/or review your goals and your plan, to review and evaluate the effectiveness of your activities and move forward on activities to help you accomplish your goals, thus achieving significantly more results than if you just played defense all the time!

When you set goals, plan out in detail how you will meet them, frequently review your progress and make corrections where necessary, you will indeed meet them.

If, on the other hand, you don't have goals, or your goals are aimlessly set, you'll easily find yourself off course, uncertain where you went astray, and unable to hit your mark. And then you'll call me. Sigh.

Here's a good and true life example of why good planning matters.

Kara is a rookie that works for me. She's often featured in my YouTube videos…a budding rockstar for sure! Kara came to me in July. She had made $42,000 so far for the year, and wanted to make $75,000 before the end of the year. We had six months.

First, how much do you LOVE a rookie leasing agent who's 23 years old and already made $42,000, but is HUNGRY to make more?!? It's a shopping center owner's dream.

Second, to help her make that goal, you have to reverse-engineer her plan.

Here's exactly how we broke it down. Let's look at Kara's example and then you can use the closing ratio formula resource box that follows.

(Note: All of these numbers are based on historical empirical data culled from tracking my own and my team's numbers throughout the years.)

Kara's Closing Ratio Formula:

- Kara's Goal: $75,000; she had already made $42,000 so she needed to earn an additional $35,000 by year's end.

- Avg. Commission/Signed Lease: $4,000

- # of Signed Leases Needed: 9

- # of Showings Needed to Get Out 9 Leases: 36 (Rookies should be looking to convert 25% of their showings into leases.)

- # of Cold Calls + Canvasses Needed to Get 36 Showings: 4,800–7,200 (Rookies should expect to show space to about ½—3/4% of the prospects they canvass/cold call)

- # of Weeks to Achieve Goal: 25

- # of Cold Calls + Canvasses/Week Needed (Avg.): 240

- # of Cold Calls + Canvasses/Day Needed (5-day week): 48

Here's where Kara was at the end of the first half.

- Signed Leases: 2

- # of Showings Held: 18

- # Cold-calls Made: 2,170 (1113 Calls; Emails sent: 432; Facebook Messages Sent: 412; Canvasses: 213)

Closing Ratio "Tracking Formula"

Use the following chart to plug in your own numbers.

Financial Goal: $_____
Average Commission per Deal $ _____

Divide these two.

Financial Goal/Average Commission = _____ deals to reach goal

Reality Check: How many deals completed last year?

_____ appointments/showings = 1 deal
_____ call ins/cold calls = 1 appointment showing

_____ calls X # _____ appointments X # _____ deals = _____ calls

_____ calls / 12 months / 20 days = _____ calls per day

Like any good "half time" coach, it's my job to look at first-half results, evaluate the analytics and use that information to help my team make the right adjustments. So, how was Kara doing? Well...

Let's do the math:

In the first three months, Kara made about 2,200 cold-calls (about 37 cold calls/day). This put Kara slightly off her target of 48 calls/day. After taking a closer, week-by-week look, it was easy to see why. During weeks 6–8, Kara was either attending the ICSC conference or helping me prepare for it. During that same period, her daily cold call average dropped significantly. After our review, Kara adjusted her daily call goal to 60 for the remaining 13 weeks. When I checked back in she was already beginning to reap the benefit with significantly more qualified leads.

Now do you get the importance of understanding, reverse engineering, and tracking metrics at every step?

But wait, there's more.

By the end of her first half, despite the slight miss on cold calls, Kara had showed space to 18 *qualified* prospects. That's a show rate of .8%, better than the .5-.75% target, and WAY BETTER than the .05% call-in rate (see Chapter 5). Kara appeared to be outperforming in how she was following up on those calls to set up showings. Way to go, Kara!

Next metric: Kara had two signed deals from those 18 showings. AHA! Me thinks we may have found the weak link in her sales chain. Typically, we can expect to convert 25% of qualified prospects to rent-paying tenants. But, Kara had only been able to convert 11%. So what did this tell me?

Either Kara was doing a poor job of "qualifying" her prospects before showings (and, if that was the case, she should re-read chapter 2) or, more likely, she was struggling with making the most of her showings. I suspected the latter.

Note to leasing managers: there is a choreography to the leasing process, especially to a showing. We can and do throw a ton of information about each step in the sales process at our rookies. It can be overwhelming; not to mention, there are some things that are just best learned experientially.

So, after your rookies have been in the field for awhile, it is important to check in. I suggest that you do the type of analysis that I did with Kara. Once you identify their challenges, you can then get out into the field with them so they can watch what you do in real time.

That's what I did with Kara. We went on "show" dates.

Once again, there really isn't any magic to this whole leasing thing. Becoming successful at it is simple, but it's not easy. That's because success always requires something from us: effort. If you're willing to do the work, the magic will usually happen.

At the time this book went to print, we were 30 days removed from both the adjustment in Kara's daily call goals and our joint showings. Not surprisingly, the compounded effect of those changes was just beginning to materialize in Kara's pay stub.

Now perhaps you're thinking at this point, "Hey Beth, that's great for Kara...but what about me? I am doing the work. I'm just not seeing the magic."

I get it. There have been times in my career (not to mention, my life) that all of my planning, my effort, and my work got me absolutely NOTHING.

When you turn the page, you'll find out about one of those times, and what I have told others to do when their efforts appear to be unrewarded.

Chapter Eight

Trouble-Shooting: What to Do When What You're "Doing" Isn't Working—And the Day I Almost Quit!

Well, you made it. You're almost to the end. Well done!

Hopefully you got to this point in my story way faster than it took me to write it down. I took 14 years to write this book.

Hopefully you've been implementing along the way and are already starting to see a difference in your results.

But what if you're not (seeing a difference)?

Maybe it's not you.

In writing this, I have realized three things:

The first is that for every sentence I put to paper, I could probably write another entire paragraph, if not chapter, on the intricacies of applying what I had just written. I guess there's another book in me.

The second is that if there is a larger, overarching, and common thread in all of my strategies it is this: internal courage combined with curiosity, humility, and persistent, deliberate action WILL pay off...

Except sometimes it doesn't, at least not when you'd like it to! Timing can matter. That was my third "aha" moment, and the inspiration for this chapter. Occasionally the best planning, the hardest work and most diligent effort will yield the most dreaded result:

Nothing.

It's happened to me. In fact, I almost quit once because of it.

True story: after three years of progressive success, I faced my first real failure test. I had just been hand-picked to work on my company's biggest project: a 400,000 square foot anchored center in a strong, suburban market that was owned by a very large institution ready to make deals.

I was hired after 100,000 square feet had blown out all at once. The center had lost ¼ of its occupancy almost overnight. By the time I took over, there had been a compounding effect. The market was spooked; the center was perceived to be jinxed.

Enter me: The Shopping Center Savior in Her Signature Red Suit.

How to Spot Rock Star Characteristics of Great Leasing Agents

What do I look for when interviewing and hiring for my team?

For starters, I like it when the person I'm interviewing wears a shirt to the interview. I'm not kidding. I did a Skype interview with a would-be social media manager and he showed up on video without a shirt! (He didn't get the job.)

On a more serious note, retail real estate leasing can be extremely lucrative, and I have seen people from all different backgrounds and experiences excel at it. Generally, what I look and test for in potential candidates is persistence, an outgoing personality, hunger to succeed and learn, humbleness, and personal accountability. I use the PI Behavioral Assessment, a Predictive Index, to help me identify "Best Fit" employees and to maximize their productivity once on board.

Also, I will probably not hire anyone who comes to the interview having not done their research or made an attempt to answer the simple questions independently. (For example, "Where are you located?" Uh, gee, have you heard of this new fangled thing called Google?) I'm looking for an appreciation for evidence-based solutions. If you come in with a whole bunch of excuses or fail to follow up after we meet, you're out for sure.

Clearly, you want to hire people who are at least invested enough to do some research, dress appropriately, and follow up. If they can't manage the basics, why would you want to put your business on the line for them?

I thought I would be the savior coming in to save the day! If only.

For the next six months, I worked harder than I ever had. I saw literally 100 prospects every single day: 50 cold calls; 50 canvasses. Every. Single. Day. For six months. You know how much space I leased in that period?

Not a single square foot.

Ever been there? If you haven't, you probably will be at some point in your life. Will you know what to do?

Me? I went to my boss, crying.

Not my finest moment, because, as you may have guessed by now, I'm not one for shedding tears. But there I was, crying with my three-ring binder full of the 13,200 prospect sheets I had collected, and ready to throw in the towel.

We reviewed my market study, my calls, my canvasses, my 13,200 sheets, my numbers.

There was nothing that stood out. No obvious course correction to be made. It was frustrating and yet somewhat comforting.

That's when my boss called the client. My boss and the client both simply encouraged me to be persistent, to keep going. They reminded me that sometimes, when you've done all the prep and all the work, it's just a matter of timing and time. In this instance, they were right.

In the next six months, I changed nothing in any material way. I, did however, lease 50,000 square feet.

It was my very first 6-figure year! Woo-*hoo*!

This time, unlike the Sir Speedy deal, I wasn't merely lucky. This time, I was prepared and persistent.

If you haven't yet had an epic fail moment or a crisis of confidence, it's probably only a matter of time. Happens to all of us. It will likely happen to me again. That's life and the law of averages.

I get calls all the time from agents in various states of angst, hoping to get a little advice or encouragement to break out of a funk, overcome an obstacle, or simply identify where to correct their course.

These calls all start the same way: with a *"Hey Beth..."*

So, I started to refer to these situations as "Hey Beth" moments.

Without further ado, here are some of the more common "Hey Beth" moments I've heard and how I've responded. Hopefully this advice will help you should you find yourself facing a "Hey Beth" moment of your own.

Here are my most popular "Hey Beth..." moments.

1. *"Hey Beth... Help! I can't lease this space."*

I get this one a lot!

"Let me guess, it's in the elbow?" I'll ask.

"How'd you know…?"

Ninety percent of unleased space is in the "elbow." It's just easier to lease end caps! It makes sense that the end caps would be easier to lease. They come with a view, which is essentially a "billboard."

That said, one of the biggest causes of elbow vacancy is that leasing agents are not properly matching their tenants' uses to the spaces they have available. End caps are for Impulse Tenants (see Resource Box for definition and examples). Elbows should be reserved for Destination Tenants. If you're having trouble leasing your elbow, first look at who is occupying your end caps. Are they the right tenants, or can they be relocated to the elbow (and save some money in the process)?

You'd be surprised at how often leasing issues are solved by properly matching your spaces with the right tenant uses. The only exception to the end cap that I would make is for a Destination Tenant who is willing to pay a premium (on the premium) for an end cap space.

The Two Types of Tenants

Do you have the right "tenant mix"?

Impulse Tenant: There are way more impulse tenants than destination tenants. They belong in your end caps because these retailers are accessories, ice-cream stores, fast casual dining, urgent care medical facilities, volume discount hair salons, jewelry stores, apparel stores, etc.

Destination Tenant: These retailers require less street-level visibility. They include places like chef-driven, iconic restaurants, education services and tutors, daycare, dentists, personal trainers, pediatricians/primary care/specialty medical doctors, printers, etc.

2. *"Hey Beth...Help! My client's rates are WAY TOO HIGH! How can I get them to be realistic?"*

Ok, there is only one way to persuade your boss, your client or your prospect that you have the right rate for the market. It's to do a PROPER market study (see also Chapter 7).

That means doing a market study that goes beyond the tired data in the usual leasing databanks. Instead, get the real intel, like rates from your leasing friends (that's why I want you to become at least Facebook friends with your peers). If you do this, you will find that you have a much more compelling case.

3. "Hey Beth…Help! I'm not a high status agent yet. I can't get any of the good spaces!"

Our #1 job as leasing agents is to "create value" for the centers that we represent. The more value that you create, the faster you'll be given the better projects. The only sure-fire way to get better space is to lease the space you got!

Maybe you've already done so, but you still haven't "moved up the food chain." If so, ask yourself if you've brought in the right deals. In other words, are you the agent who consistently brings in deals—but some of those have a lower value than budget? If that's the case, either do a careful market study of the budget (see also question #2), or take a true accounting of what you're doing.

Start with the 5 Uses Worksheet in the Appendix. Then review your metrics. Are you really working hard enough? Are you canvassing? Are you tracking your steps/metrics? Have you identified the right types of uses for your type of space? If the answer is "no," then get out there and get busy! Or… are you saying *"NO"* for your prospects?

4. "Hey Beth… Help! I can't keep track of my prospects and projects!"

I am a huge proponent of data-driven decisions! I could not do what I do without good SYSTEMS to hold and track my information. Customer Relationship Management Systems (CRM) and Project Management Systems (PM) are prerequisites to success.

There are a number of off-the-shelf systems with a variety of features and benefits. Choose one that is simple enough that you will use it, but robust enough that it adds value to your sales process. I do not recommend trying to build one to suit on your own—I have seen many companies go down this rabbit hole with nothing but debt to show for it. One thing to remember about a CRM: "if it's work... it won't work!"

5. *"Hey Beth...Help! I need a creative angle. What's the coolest thing in retail leasing that you've seen lately?"*

Shipping containers.

Chapter Nine

Investing in Your Two Most Important Assets

> *Formal Education will make you a living; self education will make you a fortune.*
>
> JIM ROHN

So, here are a few quick but insightful questions: If you were a stock, would you invest in yourself?

If so, what kind of return would you want?

Now what if I told you that you could invest 3% of your gross income and get a 28% return on that investment the next year... would you do it?

Not sold?

Then what If I told you that studies have shown that people who annually invest 3% of their gross income back into their own personal development are far more likely to reach the pinnacle of their chosen careers, and that they are more often in the top 1% of all performers in their fields?

How could you NOT make that investment?!?

It's the one investment you are guaranteed never to lose!!

In the last year alone, I spent more than $35,000 on my own self-improvement. Totally worth every penny.

And what about your team and your bench? These are the people that you are counting on (hopefully, long-term) to help you grow and expand.

Are you hiring the right people? How do you know?

What are the rock star qualities you should be looking for in a new hire? This is a question I get asked all of the time. Check out the Resource box on the following page for my full answer.

How are you bringing them into your business? Are you giving them enough training, the right tools and support?

Once they're up to speed, are they growing? Are they learning? Are they improving?

Self-improvement experts say that most employees reach a learning plateau after the first two years in a job or new position. When your staff feels they have learned all they can, they begin to coast. Which direction do you think they'll go? Which direction do you go when you're coasting?

Downhill.

I said at the outset that I am both a teacher and a learner at heart. I believe in continuous growth and development. It is both the how and the why of who I am, where I am and what I do.

Personally, I bet that I spend at least 300 hours per year learning from someone else and double that time sharing what I've learned.

(Note: A simple, FAST, and inexpensive way to start investing in yourself? Subscribe to Blinklist and read for 5 minutes per day for the next 300 days. That's 1,500 minutes of learning. Since it takes 180 minutes to finish one book, by the end of that period, you will have read 8 books. With just 5 minutes per day!)

The rest of my allocated work time I spend applying all of that acquired knowledge to my business… to implementing what I've learned.

That's what I'd like you to do right now.

Kudos to you for reading the book! BUT I'll have failed you if you don't actually use what you've learned.

So, for me… stop what you're doing right now and pick ONE THING you learned in this book and plan to add it to your "to do" list tomorrow.

Seriously. What is it? Write it down. Write down the time that you'll start. Write down what you hope to accomplish and when you plan to finish. Now, see yourself doing it.

Oh… **DON'T SAY NO.**

And finally when you've completed that one thing, send me an email with how it went. I really want to know!

Best of luck, rockstars! You got this!

Beth

by Beth's Assistant, Sidekick, and Work Wife, Josee Crosbie

How I Also Went from Rookie to Rockstar to Superstar to...INVESTOR

Beth first told me that she was going to write this book on the day that she interviewed me. That was 15 years ago.

Better late than never, right?

When we started together, Beth had just left her job and was in the very beginning stages of putting together her first major shopping center investment deal.

It didn't work out as she had envisioned.

Was Beth disappointed? Deeply. She's human. I think you learn a lot about someone when plans go awry. Beth doesn't let a defeat get in the way of future success.

Through the years and despite the occasional epic fail, we also crushed it a lot. One year we landed 20 new national retailers in our properties in just 12 months.

There was a six month period where we raised our rents by 40% across the board and our occupancy rate actually doubled!

Just this year Beth decided to "throw together" a little neighborhood awards show for mom and pop retailers. We held the first ever cause-related Retail Leasing Awards Show this past September. In true Beth fashion, this "thrown together" event was SOLD OUT, SO WELL-RECEIVED and raised $8,000 for Big Brothers & Big Sisters. It's gonna be HUGE next year.

I'm often asked if Beth ever sleeps. Or what Kool-Aid she's been drinking (and can they have some, please).

So for the record...

While I'm amazed at her mind and her energy, Beth does sleep—at least as much as any working mom with two teenage boys could sleep. As I hope that you have realized by now, there is no Kool-Aid that she's drinking or offering.

There is no one easy explanation as to why Beth has built and sustained over time and through many types of markets a business that consistently outperforms the averages. Or why she continues to innovate and launch new ventures.

What she does have is something anyone can adopt: a well-thought-out, tested, AND simple philosophy that doesn't allow her to say NO for someone else. What she does is also something anyone can do. Beth practices certain behaviors (which she describes in this book) that CONSISTENTLY and over time yield results.

Simple, but not easy to live.

Beth, like many successful people, is a visionary, a planner and a detailed implementer, though not necessarily in equal measure.

See, she is human!

What Beth has managed to do is remain humble enough to recognize when she needs help to shore up a weakness in any one of these areas.

She's also pathologically curious AND stays open to new ideas from any industry and any person and she's super responsive to even the most subtle changes afloat—whether it's a new market trend (shipping containers), new technologies, or a new skill she needs to develop or hire.

What's more, Beth consistently does everything that she advises her agents to do. She doesn't say No for her prospects. She plans. She tests. SHE CANVASSES. She tracks her results. She adjusts. Beth always has Plan A, Plan B, and even a Plan C.

AND she's a great boss and mentor. In the 15 years we've been together, Beth has not only taught me about my job, she has given me the tools (and confidence) to master the industry.

Today, I invest in all of our deals. Beth always creates a way for her employees, friends, and family to benefit if they wish to do so. That's Beth's way: abundance creates more abundance. So I own "a blade of grass" in several deals. I'm not gonna lie, I've got quite the garden growing with a chance to make a generational impact for my family. Thank you, Beth!

And much like my mentor, I want to pay this forward and give everyone a chance to have this opportunity. So now that this book has finally been put to bed, I'm begging you Beth…

"PLEASE WRITE THE NEXT ONE ON INVESTING IN RETAIL REAL ESTATE AND PLEASE DON'T LET IT TAKE YOU 15 YEARS TO DO SO!"

In the interim if you'd like to learn more about what Beth is busy doing for aspiring real estate rockstars, superstars (and would-be investors), please give me a call. I'm happy to talk to you about what's happening in our market or yours.

Thank you, Beth!

About the Authors

Beth Azor

Beth Azor is a sales coach with "Skin in the Game."

She is the founder and owner of Azor Advisory Services (AAS), a leading commercial real estate advisory and investment firm based in Southeast Florida.

Beth currently owns and manages six shopping centers in Florida and is a passive investor in several other large residential and commercial real estate projects.

Prior to founding AAS, Beth was the President of Terranova Corporation, Florida's largest third-party asset manager. Beth also has over thirty years of experience in managing, developing, redeveloping and teaching commercial real estate leasing agents. She has traveled all over the country (and Spain) lecturing and teaching other retail real estate professionals how to conquer the market by offering commercial real estate training courses and workshops. Her canvassing workshops are legendary!

A graduate of Florida State University, Beth currently serves on FSU's international program board. She previously served as a Foundation Trustee and is past Chairwoman of the Board, and Founder of the FSU Real Estate Foundation. Beth is also the immediate past President of the Board of Directors of HOPE Outreach Center in Davie, Florida and co-founder of 100+ Women Who Care in South Florida. She resides in Davie with the lights of her life, Alex and Mario.

Jill Ratzan

Beth's co-writer, Jill Ratzan, is both a business builder and a writer. Prior to launching her first business (a yoga center in South Florida), she spent 12 years with Discovery Communications, Inc. (Discovery Channel, TLC, etc.). *Don't Say NO for the Prospect* is Jill's third book project; she is also the co-author of two books on higher education.

Jill graduated from Tufts University in Medford, MA. After Tufts, Jill got her MBA from American University in Washington, DC, where she was also a Graduate Teaching Fellow in Marketing Communications.

She lives in Weston, Florida with her husband and business partner, Peter Ratzan, and their two amazing kiddos: Robyn and Isaac.

Appendix

"The rung of the ladder was never meant to rest upon, but only hold a man's foot long enough to enable him to put the other somewhat higher."

Goals Sheet

Income Goal for this coming Year _____: $ _____

Deal Goals - 5 things you are going to specifically do to get there (i.e. "Increase my canvassing to 40 new prospects per week"):

1. _____
2. _____
3. _____
4. _____
5. _____

Property Goals - List each property and what goals you have for each (i.e. "Lease 5,000sf space at Palm Harbor by April 30th.")

_____
_____
_____
_____
_____

Networking Goals - Join any committees – i.e. ICSC, Chamber of Commerce?

_____
_____
_____
_____
_____

Leadership Goals

_____
_____
_____
_____
_____

Educational Goals – i.e. CCIM, Spanish, Mandarin?

_____
_____
_____
_____
_____

"New Business" Goals

_____
_____
_____
_____
_____

Company Goals - Any ideas you have to improve something that is being done at your company?

_____
_____
_____
_____
_____

Ways to save money at _____ :

_____
_____
_____
_____
_____

Personal Goals - 2 goals (i.e. go to Hawaii, coach kids' team, etc):
1. _____
2. _____

> "Don't say you don't have enough time. You have exactly the same number
> of hours per day that were given to Helen Keller, Pasteur, Michelangelo,
> Mother Theresa, Leonardo da Vinci, Thomas Jefferson and Albert Einstein."

PROSPECTING

Beth's Prospecting Pledge

I pledge to prospect. Beginning right now, I will schedule time to prospect on a weekly basis in order to improve my income and realize my dreams.

I, _____, commit to prospecting **4 hours per week.**

I will calendar this time and not deter from this pledge.

Signature: _____

Date: _____

Beth Azor
Azor Advisory Services, Inc.
beth@azoradvisoryservices.com
Mobile: 305-970-0416

7 Easy Steps To Obtaining Franchise Disclosure Documents!

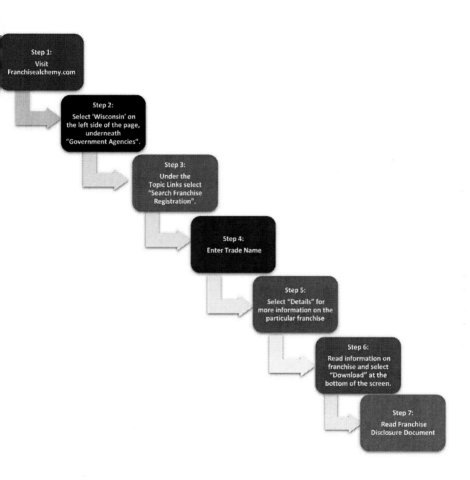

Step 1:
Visit
Franchisealchemy.com

Step 2:
Select 'Wisconsin' on the left side of the page, underneath "Government Agencies".

Step 3:
Under the Topic Links select "Search Franchise Registration".

Step 4:
Enter Trade Name

Step 5:
Select "Details" for more information on the particular franchise

Step 6:
Read information on franchise and select "Download" at the bottom of the screen.

Step 7:
Read Franchise Disclosure Document

MARKET STUDY

SHOPPING CENTER	ADDRESS	ANCHOR	OTHER TENANTS	OUTPARCELS	VACANCY	GLA	AVAILABLE SF	VACANCY %	QUOTED RATES	NNN	COMMENTS	CONTACT

Sample Canvassing Plan

Plan
- We are spending the day canvassing Middletown, NY and Kingston, NY

Goal
- Speak to 50–65 tenants (Big number, high hopes for us)
- Bring in 5–10 small shop leads

Expectations
- Positive attitude all day.
- Be energetic.
- You guys need to review and be familiar with the site plan and the rents. We are focusing on the small shop #105/ #107 and #120/#121.
- I have attached the rent table, please have an idea what the gross rents are for each of those spaces.
- I'm not expecting you guys to be pros, just focus on getting better and better after each conversation.

Materials
- 100 colored flyers
- Rent roll

Dress code
- Look good, feel good
- Business casual (Jeans w/ polo or button up)

Times
- Let's plan to leave around 8:45–8:50
- I want to be in Middletown by 9:45
- We will leave and head home once we hit our number

Get Pumped!

Canvassing plan courtesy of Christopher Ressa, DLC Management.

Closing Ratio "Tracking Formula"

Use the following chart to plug in your own numbers.

Financial Goal: $_____
Average Commission per Deal $ _____

Divide these two.

Financial Goal/Average Commission = _____ deals to reach goal

Reality Check: how many deals completed last year?

#_____ appointments/showings = 1 deal
#_____ call ins/cold calls = 1 appointment showing

#_____ calls X #_____ appointments X #_____ deals = _____ calls

#_____ calls / 12 months / 20 days = _____ calls per day

Shopping Center Name:

_____

Top 5 uses

1. _____

2. _____

3. _____

4. _____

5. _____

30 More Qualifying Questions To Ask Prospects
BEFORE YOU GIVE THE RENTAL RATES

Name: _____ Phone #: _____

Email address: _____

Type of business: _____ SF Needed: ___ Inline/OP/endcap: _____

Own Business Now: ___ If yes, how many years? __ Where: _____

What do you like about your current location?

_____

What don't you like about your current location?

_____

More than one location? ___

If yes, what makes you successful?_____

Current revenues: ___ If no, have you completed a business plan? ___

Projected first year revenues:

_____

*** What do you like about our center:

_____

Start-up capital needed: _____ Any Partners? _____

How much capital do you have? _____ Who will sign Lease? _____

Rent budget: _____ Funding sources: _____

Have you researched the area?

_____

Why do you like the area?

_____

What other areas/centers have you looked at? _____

_____

Sign needs: _____ Parking needs: _____

Tough Stuff: A Personal Guarantee is required.

Other issues that may pose as objections down the line:

_____

Beth Azor's Startup Business Plan

PROJECTIONS / STARTUP COSTS
Please complete or provide a copy of a formal business plan.

Business Name: _____

For (type of business): _____

Period (ex. year, month, etc.) : _____

EXPECTED GROSS SALES $ _____

Calculation:

_____   _____
_____   _____
_____ (A)   _____ (A)

COST OF GOODS

Calculation:

_____   _____
_____   _____
_____ (B)   _____ (B)

Net Sales: $ _____

EXPENSES

Payroll   _____
Payroll Taxes   _____
Rents   _____
Accounting   _____
Advertising   _____

Auto   _____
Contract Labor   _____
Dues/Franchise Fees   _____
Equipment Lease(s)   _____
Insurance   _____
Legal Fees   _____
Licenses   _____
Other   _____
Office   _____
Supplies   _____
Telephone   _____
Utilities   _____

TOTAL EXPENSES $ _____
EXPECTED TAXABLE INCOME $ _____

START UP COSTS
(i.e., build-out, equipment, deposit, prepaid rent, etc.) $ _____

Your qualifications to run/open business:

_____

What marketing strategies will you employ to make consumers aware
you are in the marketplace? _____

_____

"How do I get a National Retailer to respond to me?"

17 Tips Direct From The Retailers' Mouths

- Know your target. Only send centers/spaces that are appropriate for the tenant. Try to keep current on tenant's prototypes etc., so you know what works or not.

- In today's world of retail, know if tenants are getting larger or smaller. A vacant site near an existing store could mean RELO when you otherwise might write off that tenant.

- Competition map is VERY helpful, but sometimes too much detail for larger tenants is annoying. Stick to the brands/ categories and don't label EVERYTHING.

- If you must blast, you should set up different blasts based on a) SF ranges, b) target demo specifics, and c) co-tenancy anchor preferences. DO NOT SEND A 5,000 SF SPACE TO A 20,000 SF TENANT...OR A LOW-END CENTER TO A HIGH-END TENANT. IT'S A SURE WAY TO GET BLOCKED FOR GOOD.

- For ICSC meetings, giving a portfolio book is fine (but will likely end up in the trash due to carrying too much). Offer to mail it to them after the show. A nice added touch also is a flash drive of available spaces meeting that specific tenant's criteria. SHOW THAT YOU DID SOME TENANT-SPECIFIC ADVANCE PREP FOR THE MEETING.

- Don't cold call a rep you do not know about a center. Even if you know them, prep for the call before you waste their time.

- Don't email the highest senior level person info to forward to the people below them. Figure out who the current rep is (not that hard). AND FOR GOD'S SAKE, don't send ten people in the same company the same email separately, hoping one of them reacts.

- START BY CONTACTING THE LOCAL BROKER IF YOU KNOW THE NAME. Most tenants want things filtered first because they are overloaded. Copy the tenant rep as a courtesy if you wish, but don't bypass the broker. If you know the tenant wants you to screw out the broker, that is different. Beware of tenants that do this, by the way. Generally, assume the higher path is the right one, and don't be cheap. Also, don't be afraid to LIST the commission rate/amount in the LOI so the tenant knows the deal.

- If you do not have a CAD of the space, and your architectural drawings are decades old, hire a damn architect. The bigger the space, the more necessary it is that you do this. MAKE YOUR TENANTS GIVES YOU CAD FILES OF THEIR PAST BUILD OUTS....AND KEEP THEM FILED!

- There are no hard rules in most cases. You may have a space that is a bit short on width, or depth etc. Say, "I realize that it is 3' short of your required interior width, but this trade area appears to be a hole for you and your competitors. With the shortage of vacancy in this trade area, which more than meets your demographic criteria, I just wanted you to know that this space will be available soon. If you have any flexibility in your prototype design, please let me know and I will get a CAD to you ASAP. Thank you for your consideration!"

- Many retailers have real estate submittal info on their websites, so expectations have been outlined: a complete submittal package = quicker review (some retailers will not review until package is complete and/or certain minimum info is received)

- Follow submittal directions, for example:
  - ‣ some may still prefer hard copies v. electronic or vice versa
  - ‣ retailers in particular are sensitive to clicking links to access info (think security breach), some may have specific links/mail/e-mail boxes to upload info or collect submittals
  - ‣ others may want brokers to receive all info

- If you do not have a relationship with the retailer, providing a complete package promotes credibility and ensures the agent is the appropriate contact (and is purposefully seeking a particular use or tenant mix)

- Proof of control is paramount (and exclusive listing if broker is submitting)

- Do not present a space that does not even come close to the retailer's needs. A retailer told me, "I must get 2–3 calls a week from people that offer a $5K space. If they really knew 'what a great company I was,' they would know I need $75K."

- If the retailer already has a store in the market and you don't know it, this shows you didn't do your research.

- Heard from another retailer: "As far as contacting the brokers first that would be great. But to be honest, my relationship with my brokers tends to be different from region to region. I have great brokers and I have some that are not totally focused on me. So I don't mind getting the information. If I know my broker is on top of every opportunity I will let my broker handle it. If I am not sure, I will pull it up on the maps and then make sure my broker is following up. I also understand if someone does not really know who represents me in every market."

5 Ways To Crush it with Nationals at Your Next Industry Conference

Make the most of EVERY Opportunity! Beyond an initial market study, don't underestimate the power of a little preparation in every aspect of your business. This is especially true when you're trying to get appointments with national retailers at the big conferences!

Here are some pre-show tips to use to maximize your effort and your time:

1. Pick the top 20 retailers you want to meet with at the show (I know that's light for some of you, but hang with me here).

2. Check to see if they are registered. You can usually do this on the event's app or website. If you really want to get a meeting, then forget online—call them and ask if they'll be attending. Obvious, right?

3. Research the retailer. Check out their social media accounts, search hashtags with their name, search Google News for any recent articles or press releases.

4. Spend 20 minutes looking at the company's website, annual report, site submittal requirements. Then review the representative's social media. Check their LinkedIn page, Facebook page, and Twitter account if they have one. Search "Google alerts" for the representative's name and the company. (Yes, that means spending 20 min x 20 retailers = 400 minutes or almost 7 hours... Easy peasy! Do it today!)

5. When you are convinced that your property would be a good match for them by everything you read, complete and

submit a THOROUGH site submittal package and follow their package requirements completely.

6. *Only then*, request an appointment at the Conference.

7. Last tip: I do understand that your goal may be to do a full portfolio review during your meeting. If this is the case, be sensitive to their time and be transparent about your objective at the outset.

While you are doing the research, you may determine on your own that this retailer doesn't fit your property based on their requirements. You should still send the package (remember: Don't Say *NO* for them). However, communicate in the cover letter that you have done the research—and even though they have a requirement of a daytime population of "X" and you only have "Y", for this reason [insert reason here], you decided to send it anyway.

I promise you, if you put in the work, you will get the appointment. The retailers grouse all the time that we leasing agents do not do our homework. They say the ones that do put in the time to do homework get faster responses! Let's do our homework people! Prepare. Prepare. Prepare. You'll have the best show ever!

Show that you did tenant-specific prep for the meeting.

A NATIONAL RETAILER WITH 150+ LOCATIONS

Sample Ads

The following pages you'll find examples of actual local ads I have run for various types of locations:

1. A restaurant space
2. A hair salon location
3. A 1500 sq. ft. office space

128

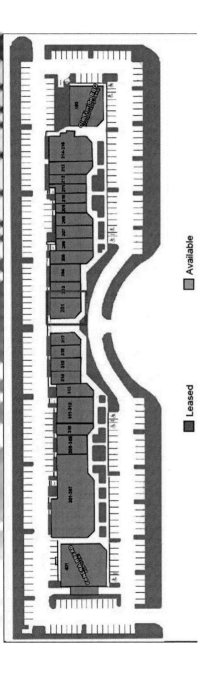

Leased Available

Bay #	Tenant	SF	Bay #	Tenant	SF
100	Old Florida Bar-B-Q (Formerly Sonny's)	3,360	214-215	Burger 21	2,913
201	AVAILABLE	1,535	301-307	AVAILABLE	7,927
202	Maggie Moo's Ice Cream	1,224	308-309	LaSpada's Original Hoagies	1,500
204	Yolanda P. Solarte, D.D.S., P.A.	1,441	310	AVAILABLE	1,175
205	South Florida Vision	1,120	311-312	Sprint	2,375
206	Distinctive Carpet & Tile	1,200	313	AVAILABLE	1,150
207	Domino's Pizza	1,200	314	Amazing Oriental Massage	927
208	AVAILABLE	1,150	315	AVAILABLE	1,000
209-210	Rising Starz Musical Academy	1,500	316	Maurice's Jewelry Box	1,000
211	Leasing Office	750	317	Avalon Hair & Nail Design	950
212	Salon Euphoria	900	400	Panera Bread	4,980
213	Twins Embroidery	1,350		TOTAL GLA	42,555

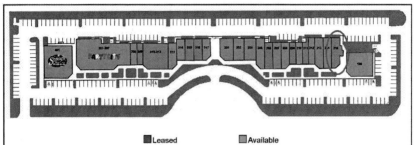

■ Leased   **■** Available

Bay #	Tenant	SF	Bay #	Tenant	SF
100	Ichiban	3,360	214	Distinctive Carpet & Tile	1,400
201	Tom Martinez Insurance Agency	1,535	215	AVAILABLE (Former Restaurant)	1,513
202	Froots	1,224	301-307	Party City	7,927
204	Yolanda P. Solarte, D.D.S., P.A.	1,441	308	LaSpada's Original Hoagies	750
205	South Florida Vision	1,120	309	AVAILABLE	750
206	AVAILABLE	1,200	310-312	AVAILABLE (Excellent Signage)	3,550
207	Domino's Pizza	1,200	313	Minuteman Press	1,150
208	All Southern Medical Supply	1,150	314	Amazing Oriental Massage	927
209	AVAILABLE	750	315	AVAILABLE	1,000
210	Rising Starz Music Academy	750	316	AVAILABLE	1,000
211	AVAILABLE	750	317	Avalon Hair & Nail Design	950
212	J. Michael Hair Salon	900	400	Sonny's Real Pit Bar-B-Que	4,908
213	EmbroidMe	1,350		TOTAL GLA	42,555

* ScanUS 2003 Estimates- No warranty or representation, expressed or implied, has been made as to the accuracy of the information provided herein, but no liability is assumed for errors or omissions.

Shoppes of Arrowhead
2411-2699 S University Dr., Davie, FL 33328

1500 sf Retail or Office Space Available!

Demographics	3 Miles	5 Miles	INCLUDES:
Population*	92,211	329,668	• Reception area
Daytime Population*	54,636	130,121	• 4 Private Offices
Average Income*	$72,974	$66,070	• Break Room
Traffic Counts: 73,000+			• Restroom

SAME PLAZA AS PANERA BREAD!   **1/4 MILE NORTH OF NOVA UNIVERSITY!**

AZOR ADVISORY SERVICES, INC.

Beth Azor
Mobile: 305-970-0416
4611 South University Dr. #110, Davie, Florida 33328
Office: 954-615-0615 * Fax: 954-615-0616
Beth@azoradvisoryservices.com

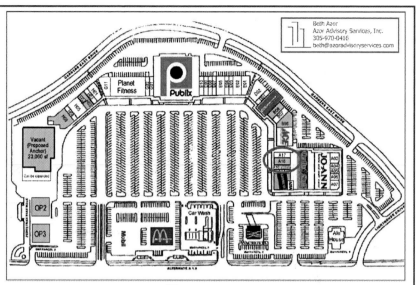

Beth Azor
Azor Advisory Services, Inc.
305-970-0416
beth@azoradvisoryservices.com

☐ AVAILABLE

Bay #	Tenant	SF	Bay #	Tenant	SF
A01	Jo-Ann Fabrics	10,609	E04	Medallion Sporting	1,700
A02	Manhattan Bagel	1,200	E05	Gardens East Wines	5,100
A04	Gardens Barber	600	E07	Promenade Animal Clinic	1,700
A05	Leasing & Management Office	600	E08	PBG Nails	1,700
A06	Drs. Eric & Arlene Jaffee	1,204	E09	Dr. Thomas Rofano	1,700
A07	Leffler Eye Care	1,632	E10	Kelly Hagar	1,700
A09	Crafts and Stuff	20,000	F	Publix	42,112
A09A	Consignment Connection	1,801	G01	Original New York Pizza	1,700
A10	Blockbuster	6,194	G02	PakMail	1,700
A14	D'Lites	1,393	G03	Planet Fitness	13,600
A15	Subway	1,310	G11	SWS Bar B Q	3,923
A16	VACANT (Former Hair Salon)	1,967	H01	Q. Ban Pot	2,660
A17	Sunset Tanning	1,060	H02	Prime Cut	1,500
B01	Ace Hardware	7,386	H03	VACANT (Former Hot Dog Restaurant)	1,900
B06	VACANT (Former Children's Play Area)	4,176	H04	Mandev	1,100
B07	Yumi Sushi	1,400	H05	Inspiration House	4,500
B08	VACANT (Former Liquor Store)	2,000	H08	Nature's Way	1,500
C	CVS Pharmacy	6,720	H09	VACANT (Former Restaurant)	5,901
D01	Sheila's	1,000	I	VACANT - PROPOSED ANCHOR	23,060
D02	Capital Carpet	4,318	OP2	VACANT	5,985
E01	Lighthouse Drycleaning	2,106	OP3	VACANT	5,985
E02	Jenny Craig	2,550	OP5	McDonald's	3,200
E03	Chopsticks House	1,700		TOTAL GLA	216,852